Sunflower

Words & Music by Paul Weller

I don't care ___
2. *(See block lyrics)*

Paul Weller   Wild Wood

Wise Publications
London / New York / Paris / Sydney / Copenhagen / Madrid

Exclusive Distributors:

Music Sales Limited
8/9 Frith Street, London W1V 5TZ, England.

Music Sales Pty Limited
120 Rothschild Avenue, Rosebery, NSW 2018, Australia.

Order No.AM91706
ISBN 0-7119-3825-3
This book © Copyright 1993 by
Wise Publications

Music arranged by Roger Day
Music processed by MSS Studios

Your Guarantee of Quality:

As publishers, we strive to produce every book
to the highest commercial standards.

The music has been freshly engraved and, whilst attempting to retain the
original running order of the album, the book has been carefully designed to
minimise awkward page turns and to make playing from it a real pleasure.

Particular care has been given to specifying acid-free, neutral-sized
paper made from pulps which have not been elemental chlorine bleached.
This pulp is from farmed sustainable forests and was produced with
special regard for the environment.

Throughout, the printing and binding have been planned to ensure a sturdy,
attractive publication which should give years of enjoyment. If your copy fails
to meet our high standards, please inform us and we will gladly replace it.

Music Sales' complete catalogue describes thousands of titles and
is available in full colour sections by subject, direct from Music Sales Limited.
Please state your areas of interest and send a cheque/postal order for £1.50 for postage to:
Music Sales Limited, Newmarket Road, Bury St. Edmunds, Suffolk IP33 3YB.

Printed in the United Kingdom by
J.B. Offset Printers (Marks Tey) Limited, Marks Tey, Essex.

SUNFLOWER

I DON'T CARE HOW LONG THIS
LASTS/WE HAVE NO FUTURE–WE
HAVE NO PAST/I WRITE THIS NOW
WHILE I'M IN CONTROL/I'LL
CHOOSE THE WORDS & HOW THE
MELODY GOES–

ALONG WINDING STREETS, WE
WALKED HAND IN HAND/AND HOW
I LONG FOR THAT SHARP WIND/TO
TAKE MY BREATH AWAY AGAIN/I'D
RUN MY FINGERS THROUGH YOUR
HAIR/HAIR LIKE A WHEATFIELD
–I'D RUN THROUGH–/THAT I'D
RUN THROUGH–

AND I MISS YOU SO–I MISS YOU
SO/NOW YOU'RE GONE, I FEEL SO
ALONE–   I MISS YOU SO

I'D SEND YOU A FLOWER– A
SUNFLOWER BRIGHT/WHILE YOU
CLOUD MY DAYS MESSING UP

MY NIGHTS/AND ALL THE WAY UP
TO THE TOP OF YOUR HEAD
SUN-SHOWER KISSES, I FELT WE
HAD–/

AND I MISS YOU SO–I MISS YOU
SO/ALL I GOTTA DO, IS THINK OF
YOU–/   & I MISS YOU SO

BABY I'M, AFRAID TO SAY WHY/
          I MISS YOU SO

CAN YOU HEAL US (HOLY MAN)

CRYSTAL WORDS, THAT HANG SO
FINE/BUT NONE WILL STOP US
FALLING/PULLING FASTER ALL
THE TIME/POWERLESS TO
WARNINGS.

IF YOU FEEL THE HAND OF GOD
CAN YOU GUIDE IT HOLY MAN?
BUT YOU ARE ONLY FLESH AND
BLOOD/WAITING TOO FOR
JUDGEMENT.

STILL SAYING! DADDY DON'T
WEEP, MOMMA DON'T CRY/
EVERYBODY GETS THEIR TIME/
DON'T BE SAD, DON'T BE BLUE–
PRAY FOR ME, I'LL DO THE SAME
FOR YOU

SPLIT THE FATHER AND THE
SON/HAND WORDS TO EASE
THEM/IN THE OTHER IS A GUN–
BAPTIZED BY FEAR, AND

IF YOU HAVE THE HAND OF GOD
CAN YOU HEAL US, HOLY MAN?/
BUT YOU ARE ONLY FLESH AND
BLOOD/WAITING TOO FOR
JUDGEMENT

STILL SAYING!/HANG ON TIGHT,
HANG ON STRONG/HOW MUCH
LONGER CAN THIS GO ON–/BUT
DON'T BE SAD, DON'T BE BLUE–
IT'S ONE MORE THING SENT TO
CONFUSE–

DADDY DON'T WEEP. MOMMA
DON'T CRY,/EVERY FEAR MUST
HAVE ITS TIME./DON'T BE SAD,
DON'T BE BLUE,/PRAY FOR ME I'LL
DO THE SAME FOR YOU.

CAN YOU BRING THE HAND OF
GOD?/CAN YOU STOP THE
KILLING?/GET US BACK TO HOPE
AND LOVE–/NEVER MORE BEEN
NEEDED–

STILL SAYING!/BLOOD'S GONE BAD,
BAD TO WORSE/WORSE TO BAD
AND BACK AGAIN–/BUT DON'T BE
SAD, DON'T BE BLUE/IT'S ONE
MORE THING SENT TO CONFUSE–
–MOMMA DON'T WEEP, DADDY
DON'T CRY/EVERY FEAR MUST
HAVE ITS TIME/DON'T BE SAD,
DON'T BE BLUE/PRAY FOR ME, I'LL
DO THE SAME FOR YOU.

WILD WOOD

HIGH TIDE–MID AFTERNOON/
PEOPLE FLY BY, IN THE TRAFFIC'S
BOOM–/KNOWING–WHERE
YOU'RE BLOWING/GETTING TO
WHERE, YOU SHOULD BE GOING

DON'T LET, THEM GET YOU
DOWN/MAKING YOU FEEL, GUILTY
ABOUT/GOLDEN RAIN, BRING YOU
RICHES/ALL THE GOOD THINGS–
YOU DESERVE NOW

CLIMBING, FOREVER TRYING/
FIND YOUR WAY OUT–OF THE
WILD, WILD WOOD/NOW THERE'S
NO JUSTICE, THERE'S ONLY
YOURSELF–/THAT YOU CAN TRUST
IN/AND I SAID–HIGH TIDE, MID
AFTERNOON/ PEOPLE FLY BY, IN
THE TRAFFIC'S BOOM–
KNOWING–WHERE YOU'RE
BLOWING/GETTING TO WHERE,.
YOU SHOULD BE GOING

DAY BY DAY, YOUR WORLD FADES
AWAY/WAITING TO FEEL–ALL THE
DREAMS THAT SAY/GOLDEN
RAIN, WILL BRING YOU RICHES/
ALL THE GOOD THINGS–YOU
DESERVE NOW–AND I SAY–/
CLIMBING, FOREVER TRYING–
/FIND YOUR WAY OUT OF THE
WILD, WILD WOOD–/YOU'RE
GONNA FIND YOUR WAY OUT–
OF THE WILD, WILD WOOD.

ALL THE PICTURES ON THE WALL

AND ALL THE PICTURES ON THE
WALL/SERVE ONLY TO REMIND
YOU OF IT ALL/THE WASTED DAYS
WE COULD HAVE LIVED/NOW
WE'RE LEFT WITH NOTHING LEFT
TO GIVE.

THERE WAS A TIME I REALLY
LOVED YOU/BUT WHEN THAT WAS
I JUST CAN'T SAY–/AS ALL THE
MEMORIES MERGE INTO ONE/AS
EACH DAY BECOMES EACH DAY

THE CLOCK HANDS TICKING ON
THE WALL/ARE JUST REMINDERS
OF IT ALL/THE WASTED DAYS WE
COULD HAVE LIVED/NOW WE'RE
LEFT WITH NOTHING LEFT TO GIVE.

WE USED TO MEET EACH OTHERS'
EYES/AN' THAT'S ALL WE'D HAVE
TO SAY–/NOW WE DON'T TALK
THAT MUCH AT ALL/THE FURTHER
OUR EYES SEEM TO STRAY

AND IN A FUNNY KIND OF WAY–/
THIS EMPTY ROOM WAS FULL ONE
DAY/FULL OF LOVE THAT WE ONCE
SHARED–NOW IT ALL LOOKS SO
BARE/THE SILENT WALLS WHOSE
CRACKS I FEEL–
BUT IS THERE ROOM TO LET THE
HATRED HEAL?

HAS MY FIRE REALLY GONE OUT?

AND WHEN I OPEN MY EYES–WILL
IT THEN BE MORNING/FIRST RAYS
OF SUMMER SUN, COMING DOWN
& SHINING

AND IF I OPEN MY HEART & SAY
ALL THAT YOU WOULD WANT/
HOLD FAITH & ALL I BELIEVE,
WILL BE THERE TO GREET ME

AND IF I OPEN MY HEAD
REMEMBER ALL THAT I SAID/HEY
BABY WHAT WILL YOU FIND–
COMING DOWN TO MEET YOU–

A LOT OF WORDS BUT NO ONE
TALKING/I DON'T WANT NO PART
OF THAT/SOMETHING REAL IS
WHAT I'M SEEKING/ONE CLEAR
VOICE IN THE WILDERNESS

AND PUT AN END TO ALL YOUR
DOUBTS–/HAS MY FIRE REALLY,
REALLY GONE OUT?

COUNTRY

I KNOW A PLACE NOT FAR FROM
HERE/WHERE LIFE'S SWEET
PERFUME FILLS THE AIR/AND IF
YOU WANT I'LL TAKE YOU THERE/
IF YOU WANT I'LL TAKE YOU
THERE.

INTO THE LIGHT OUT OF THE
DARK/WHERE ONLY LOVE CAN
HEAL YOUR HEART/ AND IF YOU
WANT I'LL MAKE A START/ IF YOU
WANT I'LL MAKE A START–

THIS PLACE I SAY, HALF HOUR
AWAY/IS THAT SO FAR TO GO? SO
NEAR–/AND FURTHER ON WE'LL
FIND THE TIME/AND LOSE THE
DISCONTENT WE FEEL–THAT WE
FEEL

I FEEL THE TIME WE'VE YET TO
REACH/IS NOT YET WITHIN OUR
BELIEF/BUT I FEEL SURE THAT
TIME WILL COME/IF IT GOES ON
AT ALL–IF IT GOES ON AND ON–/
IF IT GOES ON AND ON–

I KNOW A PLACE NOT FAR FROM
HERE/WHERE LIFE'S SWEET
PERFUME FILLS THE AIR/ AND IF
YOU WANT WE'LL LAY A WHILE
THERE–/IF YOU WANT WE'LL LAY
A WHILE THERE.

5TH SEASON

A STORM IS RAGING, INSIDE MY
HEAD/THE WIND IS HOWLING,
SUCH THOUGHTS OF DEATH/WHY
AM I SO LOST AND CONFUSED/
CAN'T FIND THE REASON, FOR
FEELING BLUE/THERE'S SO MUCH
I CAN'T EXPLAIN/HOPE THIS
SEASON CHANGES SOON.

THE LIGHTNING STRIKES AND THE
MOUNTAINS FALL/THE SEA'S
COME CRASHING, AGAINST IT
ALL/HANG ON TIGHT, IN THE
TIDES OF CHANGE/AND GET YOUR
BEARINGS FROM THOSE STILL
SANE/THERE'S SO MUCH I'VE YET
TO FEEL/HOPE THE SEASONS
CHANGE ME TOO.

THE SERPENT TANGLES, IN THE
LION'S CLAW/A CLOUD OF DARK-
NESS, HANGS OVER ALL/AS FIRES
SOAR, IN SEARCH OF SKY/SO BLOW
EMBERS, LIKE FIRE FLIES/HOPING
LOVE IS WHERE THEY'LL LIE/AND
THE SEASON CHANGE US TOO.

THE WEAVER

CAN YOU PUT A SMILE BACK ON–
ALL THESE DIFFERENT FACES/OF
ALL THE PEOPLE FROM SUCH
DIFFERENT PLACES–/AND IF YOU
CAN SUCCEED, WHAT THEN WILL
YOU ACHIEVE./WITH A DIFFERENT
TUNE TO PLAY–YOU'VE BEEN
SAVING FOR A RAINY DAY

WILL YOU HEAL THE SCAR THAT'S
ON–THE YEARS BEEN WASTED/
THE TEARS SPENT OF THE PAST–
JUST FILLING SPACES–/OR IS
LOVE FOREVER GONE, BANISHED
TO A SMALLER PART,/HIDE
BEHIND YOUR WALL & START–
    TO GET TO THE VERY HEART.

AN' IF YOU WANNA SHOOT THE
MOON–MAKE SURE THAT YOU
KNOW WHY/CAREFUL, FLY TOO
SOON–BETTER LET SOMEONE
ELSE TRY–

I'M THE WEAVER OF YOUR
DREAMS–I GET RID OF YOUR
BOGEYMAN/I'M HERE TO SMASH
THE SHELL YOU'RE UNDER–/
    AN' GET YOU INTO
ANOTHER THING–

I'M THE WEAVER OF YOUR
DREAMS–I PUT PAID TO THE
ROCKET MEN/I'M HERE TO BREAK
THE SPELL YOU'RE UNDER–/
    & GET YOU STARTED
WITH ANOTHER PLAN

COULD YOU PUT A KISS BACK ON–
THE LIPS SO TWISTED/WAITING
FOR THE CHANCE TO START–
DIPPING INTO WISHES–/OR IS
LOVE FOREVER GONE, BANISHED
TO A SMALLER PART,/HIDE
BEHIND YOUR WALL AND START–
    TO GET TO THE VERY HEART.

AND IN THE MIDST OF THE
DARKEST NIGHT–/THINK OF ME
& HOLD ME TIGHT–/SO THAT I
MIGHT LIVE TO SEE–/
ALL THE WEAVING OF MY DREAMS.

FOOT OF THE MOUNTAIN

LIKE A DREAM ON THE
OCEAN/ALWAYS DRIFTING
AWAY/AND I CAN'T CATCH UP/SHE
JUST SKIPS AWAY-ON THE TIDE

SOMETIMES A GREAT NOTION/CAN
LEAD YOU AWAY/SO WEAK TO
DEVOTION/   SO STRONG TO
DESIRE.

BABY, BABY, BABY WON'T YOU LET
ME RIDE/TAKE ME OFF ON YOUR
SAIL BOAT RIDE/COME ON NOW
ANGELS, ARE ON YOUR SIDE/
BUT SHE SLIPS AWAY – /
OH & NEVER STAYS

LIKE MERCURY GLIDING/A SILVER
TEARDROP THAT FALLS/& I WILL
NEVER HOLD HER/THROUGH MY
FINGERS, SHE'S GONE.

AT THE FOOT OF THE
MOUNTAIN/SUCH A LONG WAY TO
CLIMB/HOW WILL I EVER GET UP
THERE –/   THOUGH I
KNOW I MUST TRY

BABY. BABY, BABY WON'T YOU LET
ME RIDE/TAKE ME OFF ON YOUR
SAIL BOAT RIDE/COME ON NOW
ANGELS, ARE ON YOUR SIDE/
BUT SHE SLIPS AWAY – /
OH & NEVER STAYS

LIKE A DREAM ON THE
OCEAN/ALWAYS DRIFTING
AWAY/AND I CAN'T CATCH UP/SHE
JUST SKIPS AWAY–ON THE TIDE

SHE JUST SLIPS AWAY–ON THE
TIDE/SKIPS AWAY – AS SHE GLIDES

SHADOW OF THE SUN

DO YOU STILL FEEL THE SAME
WAY ABOUT IT/LIKE YOU ALWAYS
SAID YOU WOULD/OR HAS TIME
RE-WRITTEN EVERYTHING/LIKE
YOU NEVER DREAMT IT COULD

REMEMBER WHEN WE WANTED
TO FLY FOREVER/ON A MAGIC
CARPET RIDE/WELL FOREVER
SEEMS A LONG TIME–CUTTING
US DOWN IN SIZE/NO MATTER
HOW HARD WE TRY–

AND I COULD SEE ALL I HAD DONE
JUST CHASING DREAMS ACROSS
THE FIELDS–IN THE SHADOW OF
THE SUN–

ONCE UPON A TIME I MIGHT HAVE
TOLD YOU/BUT NOW NOTHING
SEEMS THAT PLAIN/HOWEVER
MUCH WE'RE CHANGING–
THERE ARE SOME THINGS THE
SAME–/AND THOSE SAME THINGS
STILL SAY–

AND I COULD SEE ALL I HAD DONE
JUST CHASING DREAMS ACROSS
THE FIELDS–IN THE SHADOW OF
THE SUN–

I PLAN TO HAVE IT ALL WHILE I'M
STILL YOUNG/AND CHASE THE
FIELDS ACROSS MY DREAMS–/IN
THE SHADOW OF THE SUN–
IN THE SHADOW OF THE SUN

MOON ON YOUR PYJAMAS

WAS THAT A SHOOTING STAR I
SAW/IT'S RARE FOR ME TO MAKE A
WISH AT ALL/ BECAUSE I FEEL
THAT I CAN ONLY HOPE/ THESE
DANGEROUS TIMES, WE ARE
BARELY AFLOAT–

AND I HOPE THE WORLD WILL
HEAL ITSELF/AND OUR WORN OUT
SOULS ALONG WITH IT–/SO THAT
YOU WILL GET THE CHANCE TO
SAY/THAT YOU HAVE SEEN A
BETTER DAY–

YOU'VE GOT THE MOON ON YOUR
PYJAMAS/AND THE STARS IN YOUR
EYES–/SWEET CHILD YOU'RE A
DREAM IN DISGUISE–/ANGELS
ON SILVER STRINGS HANG FROM
ABOVE/LET LOVE AND LAUGHTER
SHINE WHEREVER YOU GO.......

THROUGH YOUR NEW EYES I'VE
COME TO SEE/HOW BEAUTIFUL,
MY LIFE CAN BE/ AND I'LL KEEP
THIS WISH THIS TIME I THINK
 AND BLOW IT IN WITH A KISS
UPON YOUR HEAD–

AND I HOPE THE WORLD WILL
HEAL ITSELF/AND OUR WORN OUT
SOULS ALONG WITH IT

SO THAT YOU WILL GET THE
CHANCE TO SEE/ A SUMMER'S
BLUE SKY BEING GREEN TREES–

YOU'VE GOT THE MOON ON YOUR
PYJAMAS/THE STARS IN YOUR
EYES–/SWEET CHILD YOU'RE A
DREAM IN DISGUISE–ANGELS
ON SILVER STRINGS HANG FROM
ABOVE/LET LOVE AND LAUGHTER
SHINE WHEREVER YOU GO..........

now you're gone   I   feel so a - lone, _____

oh _____   I   miss you so. _____

But   I

miss you so,   and I miss you so

now you're gone   I feel so a - lone, ___

oh ___   I miss you so. ___

Verse 2:
Along winding streets we walked hand in hand,
And how I long for that sharp wind to take my breath away again.
I'd run my fingers through your hair,
Hair like a wheatfield, I'd run through.

Verse 3:
I'd send you a flower - a sunflower bright,
While you cloud my days, messing up my nights.
And all the way up to the top of your head,
Sun-shower kisses I felt we had.

Can You Heal Us (Holy Man)

Words & Music by Paul Weller

1. Crys-tal words that hang so fine, _____ but none will stop us fall-ing. _____
2. Split the Fath-er and the Son, _____ hand words to ease _ them _

Pull-ing fast-er all the time _____ pow-er-less to warn-ings. _
in the oth-er is a gun, _____

Bap-tised by fear and _____ If you feel the hand _ of God, _
If you have the hand _ of God, _

one more thing sent to con- fuse. _ Dad- dy don't _ weep, _ Mom- ma don't cry, _

ev- 'ry fear must have its time. _ Don't be sad, don't _ be _ blue, _

pray for me, I'll do the same for _ you. _____

Lyric on D.S.
Can you bring the hand of God,
Can you stop the killing?
Get us back to hope and love,
Never more been needed.
Still saying

Blood's gone bad, bad to worse
Worse to bad and back again.
But don't be sad, don't be blue,
It's one more thing sent to confuse.
Momma don't weep, daddy don't cry,
Every fear must have its time.
Don't be sad, don't be blue,
Pray for me, I'll do the same for you.

Wild Wood

Words & Music by Paul Weller

1. High tide, — mid-af-ter-noon,
(other verses - see block lyric)
peo- -ple fly by in the traff-ic's boom. —

Verse 2:
Don't let them get you down,
Making you feel guilty about
Golden rain will bring you riches,
All the good things you deserve now.

Verse 3:
Climbing, forever trying,
Find your way out of the wild wild wood.
Now there's no justice,
You've only yourself that you can trust in.

Verse 4:
And I said high tide, mid-afternoon,
People fly by in the traffic's boom.
Knowing just where you're blowing,
Getting to where you should be going.

Verse 5:
Day by day your world fades away,
Waiting to feel all the dreams that say,
Golden rain will bring you riches,
All the good things you deserve now.

All the Pictures on the Wall

Words & Music by Paul Weller

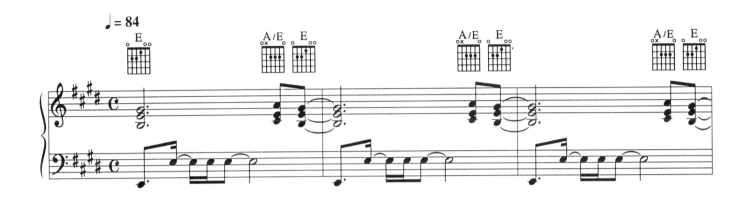

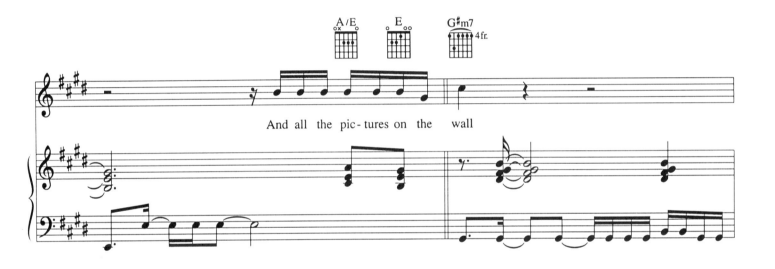

And all the pic - tures on the wall

serve on - ly to re - mind you of ___ it all.

As all the me-mo-ries merge in-to one,
Now we don't talk that much at all, _____

as each day be-comes each day. _____
the further our eyes seem _ to stray. _____

The clock hands tick - ing on the (1.3) wall, _____
and all the pic - tures on the (2) wall _____

Coda

D.%.al Coda

The clock hands tick-ing on the

Instrumental (pt 1)

Music by Paul Weller, Brendan Lynch & Steve White

Has My Fire Really Gone Out?

Words & Music by Paul Weller

And if I o - pen my head _____ re - mem - ber all that we said.

Hey ba - by what will you find com - ing down to meet you?

A lot of words but no - one talk - ing, I don't want no part of that. _____

Some - thing real is what I'm seek - ing, one clear voice in the wil - der - ness. _____

30

(Vocal 1° only) Some-thing real is what I'm seek - ing, one clear voice in the wil - der - ness.

Repeat ad lib.

(x3)

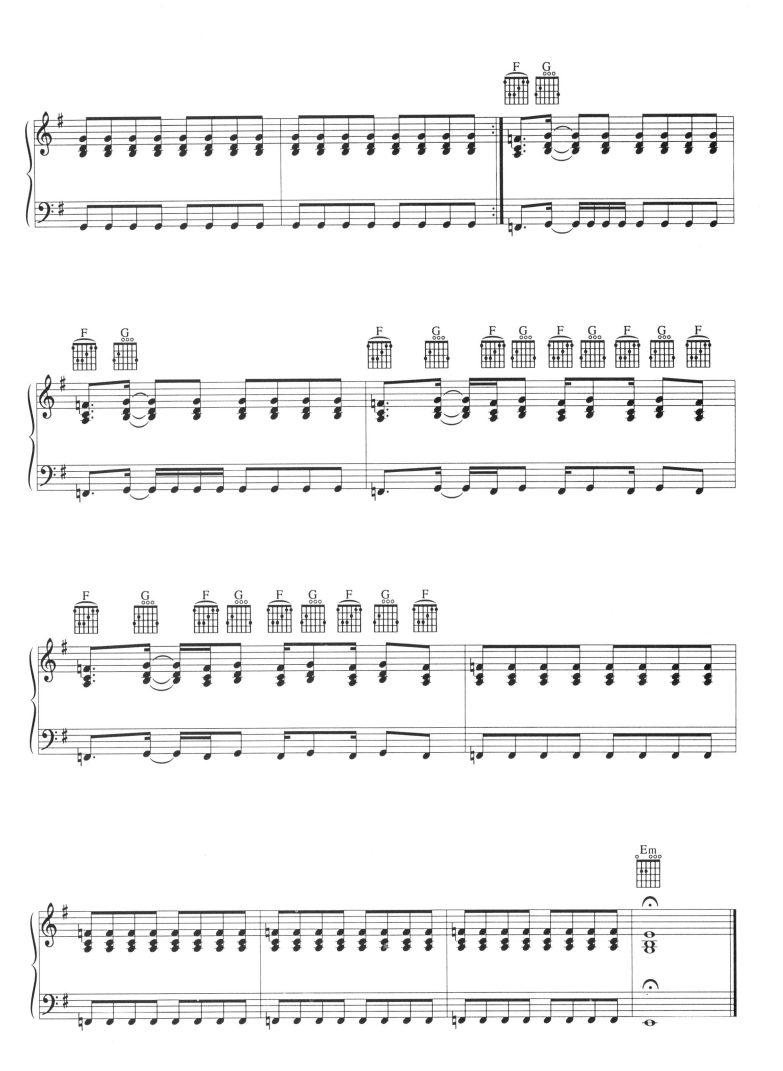

Country

Words & Music by Paul Weller

1. I know a place not far from here
2.3. *(see block lyric)*

where life's sweet per-fume fills the air.

And if you want I'll take you there,

and lose the dis - con - tent _ we feel, _____ that _ we feel.

Verse 2:
Into the light out of the dark,
Where only love can heal your heart.
And if you want I'll make a start,
If you want I'll make a start.

Verse 3:
I know a place not far from here
Where life's sweet perfume fills the air.
And if you want we'll lay a while there,
If you want we'll lay a while there.

Instrumental Two

Music by Paul Weller

5th Season

Words & Music by Paul Weller

Moderate beat

1. A storm is rag - ing in - side my
2.3. *(see block lyric)*

head, __ the wind is howl - ing such thoughts of

death. __ Why am I so lost __ and con -

fused?   can't _ find the rea - son   for feel - ing

blue. ____   There's so much ____ I can't _ ex - plain ____

hope this sea - son chan - ges soon.

(2.4.) The light-ning strikes

Verse 2 & 4:
The lightning strikes and the mountains fall,
The sea's come crashing against it all.
Hang on tight in the tides of change
And get your bearings from those still sane.
There's so much I've yet to feel,
Hope the seasons change me too.

Verse 3:
The serpent tangles in the lion's claw,
A cloud of darkness hangs over all.
As fires soar in search of sky,
So blow embers like fireflies.
Hoping love is where they'll lie,
And the season change us too.

The Weaver

Words & Music by Paul Weller

1. Can you put a smile back on
2.3. *(see block lyric)*

all these diff-'rent fa - ces of all the peo - ple from such diff-'rent pla - ces.

And if you can suc - ceed _ what then will you ach - ieve? With a diff-'rent tune _ to play,

1. you've been sav - ing for a rain - y day. _____

2. to get to the ve - ry heart. _

And if you ___ to get to the ve-ry heart. _

And if you wan-na shoot the moon, make sure that you know why. _

Care-ful, fly too soon, _ bet-ter let some-one else try. _ I'm the wea-ver of your dreams,

I get rid of your bo-gey-man. _____ I'm here to smash the shell _ you're un - der,

and get you in to an-oth-er thing.

I'm the wea-ver of your dreams,

I put paid to the rock-et men,

I'm here to break the spell you're un-der

and get you start-ed with an-oth-er plan.

And in the midst of the darkest night, ___ think of ___ me and hold ___ me tight.

So that I might live ___ to see ___ all the wea-ving of ___ my dreams. ___

Vocal Tacet 2° I'm the wea-ver of your dreams, ___ I get rid of your bo-gey-man. ___

I'm here to smash the shell ___ you're un - der, and get you in to an-oth-er thing. ___

Verse 2:
Will you heal the scar that's on the years been wasted,
The tears spent of the past, just filling spaces.
Or is love forever gone, banished to a smaller part?
Hide behind your wall and start to get to the very heart.

Verse 3:
Could you put a kiss back on the lips so twisted?
Waiting for the chance to start dipping into wishes.
Or is love forever gone, banished to a smaller part.
Hide behind your wall and start to get to the very heart.

Instrumental (pt 2)

Music by Paul Weller, Brendan Lynch & Steve White

Foot of the Mountain

Words & Music by Paul Weller

Take me off ___ on your sail - boat ride. ___ Come on now an - gels ___ are

on your side, ___ but she slips ___ a - way ___ oh and nev - er stays.

Verse 2:
Like mercury gliding,
A silver teardrop that falls.
And I will never hold her,
Through my fingers she's gone.
As the foot of the mountain,
Such a long way to climb.
How will I ever get up there,
Though I know I must try.

Holy Man (Reprise)

Words & Music by Paul Weller

Yea, he is call-ing me, ___ yea, ___ he is call-ing me, ___

yea, he is call-ing me, ___ can you hear this ho-ly man? ___

Can you hear this ho - ly man? ___

Can you hear this ho - ly man? ___

Can you hear this ho - ly man? ___

Can you hear this ho - ly man? ___

Shadow of the Sun

Words & Music by Paul Weller

1. Do you still feel __ the same __ way a-bout __ it,

like you al - ways said you would. __

Or has time __ re-writ - ten ev-

in the sha-dow of ___ the sun. ___

Moon on Your Pyjamas

Words & Music by Paul Weller

And I hope the world will heal it - self,_____ and our worn out souls a -

long with it._____ So that you'll get the chance to say_____

that you have seen _____ a bet - ter day. _____

You've got the moon on your py - ja - mas and the

stars in your eyes, _____

sweet child, you're a dream in dis - guise. _____

An - gels on sil - ver strings, hang from a - bove, ___

let love and laugh - ter shine wher - ev - er you go. _____

Verse 2:
Through your new eyes I've come to see
How beautiful my life can be.
And I'll keep this wish this time I think,
And blow it in with a kiss upon your head.

And I hope the world will heal itself
And our worn out souls along with it.
So that you will get the chance to see
A summer blue sky behind green trees.

1/96 (23254)